OUR STORY

HOW WE BECAME A FAMILY

DONOR CONCEPTION NETWORK

Text by Nina Barnsley and Stephanie Clarkson
Illustrations by Gabi Froden
Editing and Project Management by Stephanie Clarkson
Designed by Andy Archer
Produced by the 38a The Shop www.38atheshop.com
Published by the Donor Conception Network

Acknowledgements

The Donor Conception Network would like to thank the April Trust for their support in the production of these new **Our Story** books. We would also like to acknowledge Angela Mays and Jane Offord who wrote the inspirational **My Story** for sperm donation families in 1991 which was so important in helping families to be open with their children.

ISBN: 978-1-910222-65-2

Our Story 009 HCSD1

My name is:

....

I was born on:

....

This is the story of my family.

Before I was born, Mummy and Daddy loved each other very much.

One day, they decided they wanted
a baby to love and look after.

Mummy and Daddy tried to have a baby and they were sad when it didn't happen.

What could they do? Who could help?

They decided to go to see the doctor.

CLINIC

To make a baby you need a seed from a man, an egg from a woman and a nice warm tummy to grow the baby in.

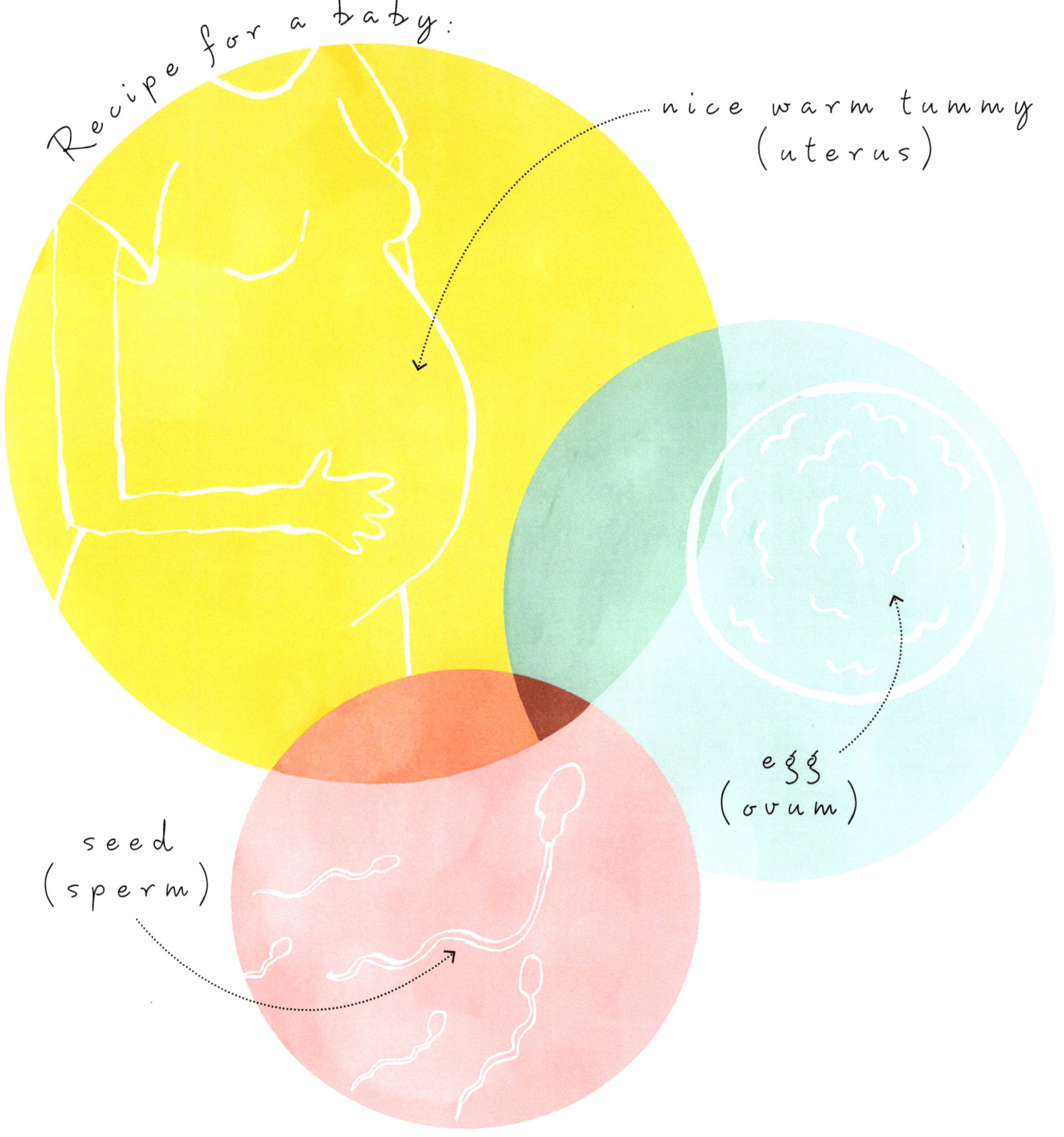
Recipe for a baby:
nice warm tummy
(uterus)
egg
(ovum)
seed
(sperm)

The doctor explained that there were problems with Daddy's seeds, which meant a baby couldn't grow.

This news made Mummy and Daddy feel very sad.

Then the doctor told them there
was still a way for them to have a baby,
but they would need some extra help.

There are men who give some of their seeds to help other people make a baby. They are called donors.

Lots of different people choose to be donors because they want to do something kind and help people like Mummy and Daddy to have children.

Mummy and Daddy were really happy to hear that there was a way they could have a baby to love.

They decided to give it a try.

CLINIC

When the time was right,
they went to the clinic. The doctor
put the donor's seed together
with Mummy's egg in her tummy.

Then they had to wait to see
if a baby would grow...

And guess what!

A baby did grow.

That baby was me!

After many months of growing
I was ready to be born.

Mummy and Daddy were
so pleased and excited to meet
me and hold me at last.

Family and friends came to
welcome me and say hello.

There are many different ways that families are made and they come in all shapes and sizes.

This is how I began and how
my family was made.

It is our story.

Here is a picture of us together.

Mummy and Daddy are very proud
of our family and they are so grateful
to everyone who helped make me.

Add a photo of
your family here.

www.ingramcontent.com/pod-product-compliance
Lightning Source LLC
LaVergne TN
LVHW070205110826
845147LV00002B/506

* 9 7 8 1 9 1 0 2 2 2 6 5 2 *